I0816443

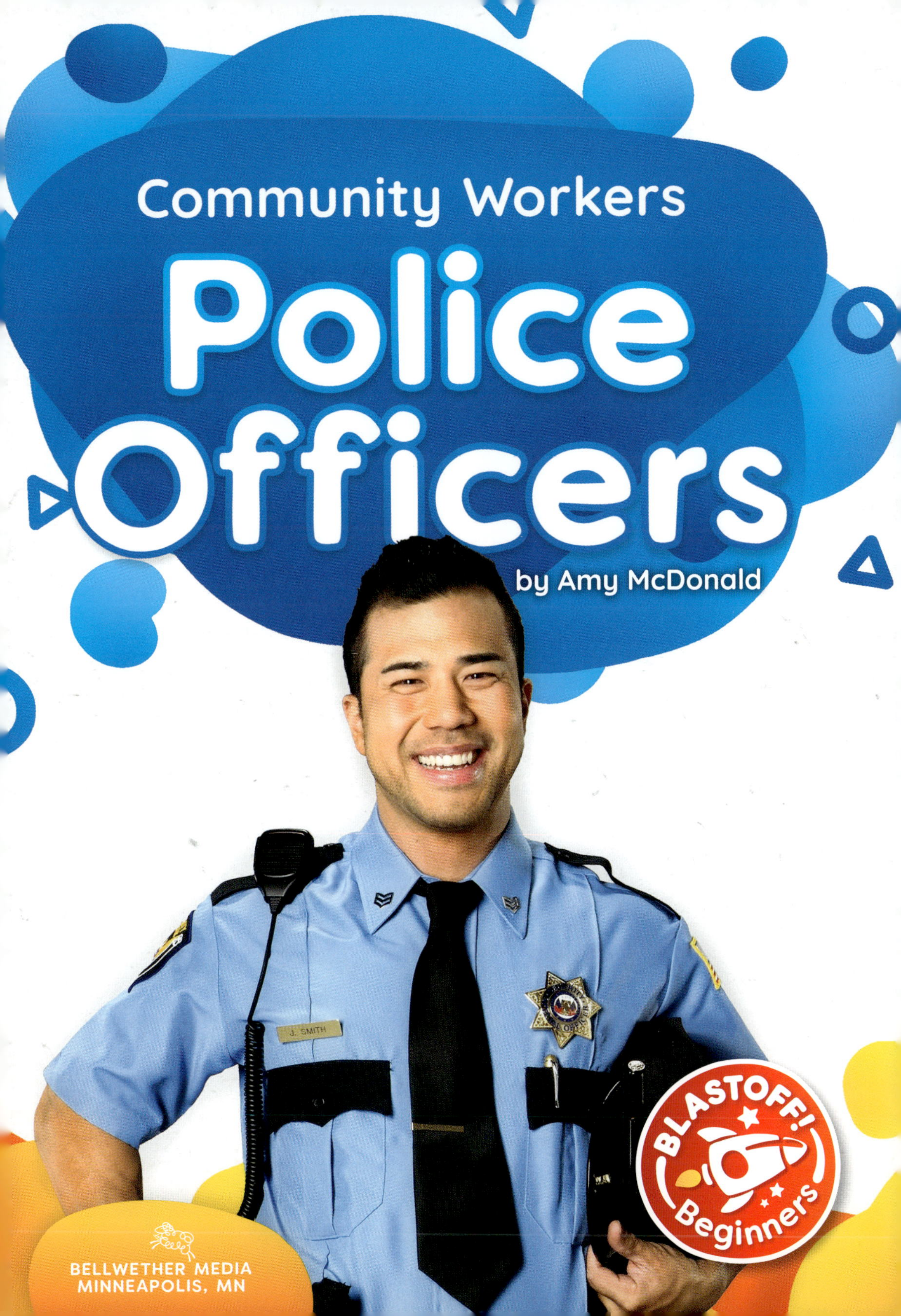
Community Workers
Police Officers
by Amy McDonald
J. SMITH
BLASTOFF! Beginners
BELLWETHER MEDIA
MINNEAPOLIS, MN

Blastoff! Beginners are developed by literacy experts and educators to meet the needs of early readers. These engaging informational texts support young children as they begin reading about their world. Through simple language and high frequency words paired with crisp, colorful photos, Blastoff! Beginners launch young readers into the universe of independent reading.

Sight Words in This Book

are	in	ride	to
go	is	some	way
have	make	the	where
help	on	there	
here	people	they	

This edition first published in 2025 by Bellwether Media, Inc.

Library of Congress Cataloging-in-Publication Data

LC record for Police Officers available at: https://lccn.loc.gov/2024004949

Editor: Betsy Rathburn Designer: Laura Sowers

Printed in the United States of America, North Mankato, MN.

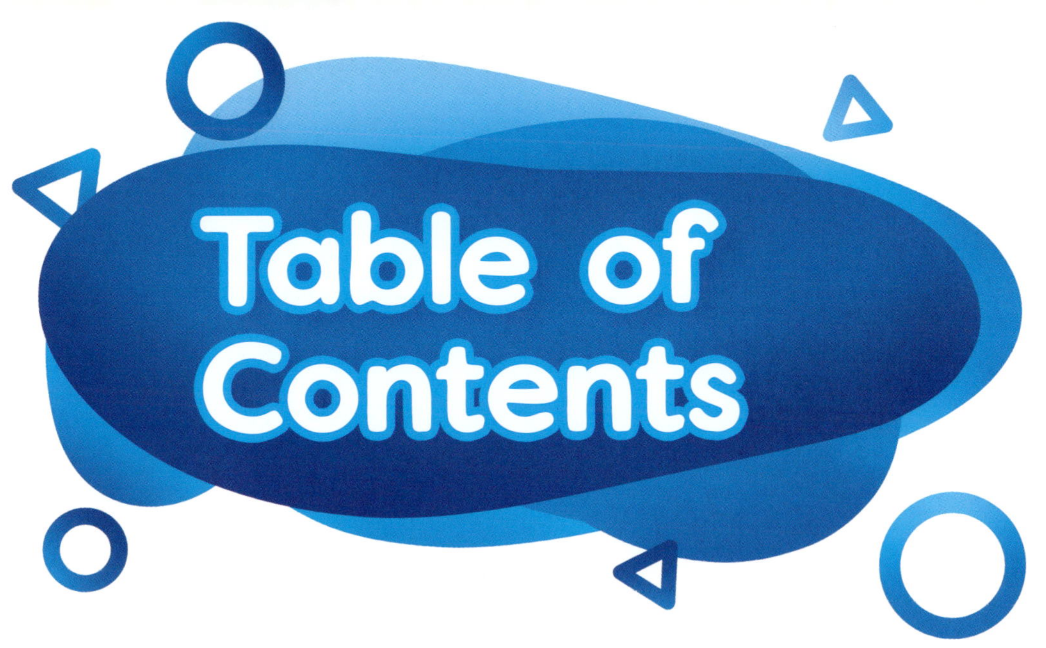
Table of Contents

SPECIAL
POLICE

On the Job

Someone needs help! Police officers are on the way.

SHERIFF
SHERIFF

What Are They?

Police officers are hard workers. They keep people safe.

SHERIFF
DEPT

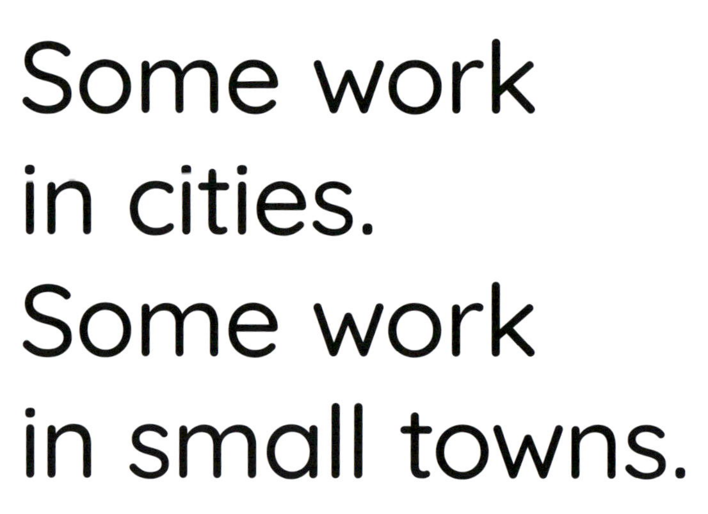

Some work
in cities.
Some work
in small towns.

LICE
LOS ANGELES POLICE
POLICE

What Do They Do?

They wear **uniforms**. They have badges.

uniform

They drive
police cars.
Some ride bikes.
Some ride horses.

MINNEAPOLIS POLICE
POLICE
TREK

They make sure people follow **laws**.

NY

They give **tickets**. They **arrest** people.

ticket
LOS ANGELES POLICE

They go where there is trouble.

POLICE
PROTECT
SERVE

Why Do We Need Them?

Police officers are here to help!

POLICE

Police Officer Facts

Tools

A Day in the Life

drive police car

make sure people follow laws

give tickets

Glossary

arrest

to take into police control

laws

rules that must be followed

tickets

notices to pay money for breaking the law

uniforms

clothes worn by police officers

To Learn More

ON THE WEB

FACTSURFER

Factsurfer.com gives you a safe, fun way to find more information.

1. Go to www.factsurfer.com.
2. Enter "police officers" into the search box and click 🔍.
3. Select your book cover to see a list of related content.

Index

The images in this book are reproduced through the courtesy of: LifetimeStock, front cover; omphoto, p. 3; Straight 8 Photography, p. 4; Colleen Michaels, pp. 4-5; RyanJLane, pp. 6-7; anouchka, pp. 8-9; PhotoVrStudio, p. 10 (badge); betto rodrigues, pp. 10-11; Leonard Zhukovsky, p. 12; miker, pp. 12-13; carstenbrandt, pp. 14-15; sirtravelalot, p. 16 (arrest); Ryan Fletcher, pp. 16-17; avid_creative, pp. 18-19; Luis Molinero, p. 20; kali9, pp. 20-21, 22 (make sure people follow laws), 23 (uniforms); Sean Locke Photography, p. 22 (uniform); Emu125, p. 22 (badge); Wangkun Jia, p. 22 (police car); inhauscreative, p. 22 (drive police car); Lisa F. Young, p. 22 (give tickets); ftwitty, p. 23 (arrest) Andrey_Popov, p. 23 (laws); bymuratdeniz, p. 23 (tickets).